LATER ELEMENTARY TO EARLY INTERMEDIATE

FAVORITE

BOOK 2

FESTIVAL SOLOS

10 GREAT NFMC SELECTIONS

T0081554

The **National Federation of Music Clubs (NFMC)** is a non-profit philanthropic music organization whose goal is to promote American music, performers, and composers through quality music education and supporting the highest standards of musical creativity and performance.

ISBN 978-1-4803-4167-8

WILLIS MUSIC

EXCLUSIVELY DISTRIBUTED BY

HAL•LEONARD®
CORPORATION
7777 W. BLUEMOUND RD. P.O. BOX 13819 MILWAUKEE, WI 53213

Visit Hal Leonard Online at
www.halleonard.com

CONTENTS

PERFORMANCE NOTES FROM THE COMPOSERS

EDITOR'S NOTE: Special thanks to Glenda Austin for providing notes on the Gillock pieces.

GOING BAROQUE / Glenda Austin
NFMC 1998-2000

Despite my playful title, the piece was created with truly Baroque characteristics. The right hand plays a single-line melody of fragmented scale passages, while the left hand keeps a steady beat in a half-note rhythm. In the middle section (measures 9-16), there is also a Baroque-like rhythmic and melodic sequence that occurs. Observe the fingering carefully to achieve fluidity in the eighth-note passages.

EVENING LAMENT / Randall Hartsell
NFMC 1998-2000

I truly believe that music sustains the human spirit through the challenges of life. My hope is that the title of this piece, combined with the E Minor key signature, will help to create an effective texture for sensitive, expressive playing. An equal balance between the hands will support nuanced melodic changes. Take note of the *tenuto* marks in the bass clef which reinforce an inner voicing. Momentum in slower pieces can be achieved by playing with a rich, full tone and utilizing a wide range of dynamics.

ON THE CHAMPS-ÉLYSÉES / William Gillock
NFMC 1998-2000

One of the most beautiful and famous streets in the world, the title fits this Gillock piece perfectly. Note the directive, "With a steady dance beat and minimal rhythmic nuance." I interpret this as playing with no *rubato*. Once you begin and set a steady tempo, it should remain constant. It may help to think of it this way: if you are driving down the Champs-Élysées, there is no room for stopping, starting, slowing or speeding—you are in the thick of it and must go with the flow! The dynamics are simple but effective, so observe them carefully. I know Mr. Gillock traveled to Paris and loved the city. I am sure he was inspired by the sidewalk cafés, fashionable stores, and beautiful architecture that line this famous street.

LITTLE WALTZ / Carolyn Miller
NFMC 2008-2010

This waltz starts with a single-note melody and gradually builds. When I play it, I imagine a prince and princess dancing in a ballroom. They are light on their feet and move gracefully in large circles. As you play, feel the beat and make your fingers do the dancing. Look for a pattern in the Coda, and end it with a big flourish (no *ritardando*)!

FOUNTAIN SQUARE / Eric Baumgartner
NFMC 2004-2006

This piece should evoke sounds and images of a gently flowing fountain set in an idyllic town park. To achieve this mood, strive for smooth, subtle dynamic and tempo changes. Be careful not to make the changes too abrupt as that could spoil the mellow mood. Do your best to keep the eighth notes even; however, 'lean' slightly on the left-hand notes to emphasize the octave jumps on beats one and three.

BLACK CAT BOUNCE / Glenda Austin

NFMC 2001-2003

We used to have a black cat. He sauntered around like he owned the place. That's exactly how this piece should sound: cool and collected! You don't have to play it quickly for it to be effective: simply observe the swing rhythm of the eighth notes, and make sure the half notes in the left hand are steady and on the beat! This is a "walking bass," which should give it a cool, beatnik feel. In the B section (measures 21-24), exaggerate the accented notes to achieve a syncopated jazz sound. And in the Coda, start softly before gliding to a big, abrupt ending.

WISTFUL CHANT / Alexander Peskanov

NFMC 1998-2000

Wistful Chant was inspired by Gregorian chant, which I studied in music literature class at the Odessa Conservatory. My fascination with the architecture and music of the 9th and 10th centuries led me to compose a melody based on the Aeolian mode (also known as the natural minor). The melodic line in the right hand consists of a two-note motif, which alternates between smaller and larger intervals, sometimes leading into a cascade of descending, scale-like passages. The repetition of these patterns creates a meditative, solemn mood. The left hand is split between two voices, providing a harmonically mysterious background. The four-measure theme that starts the piece reoccurs several times throughout, always expanding in range and sound. At the end, the listener hears only half the theme as it descends from the middle register to the bass, triggering a sense of sadness and nostalgia.

DANCE IN E MINOR / Carolyn Miller

NFMC 1995-1997

This is a fun, energetic dance with lots of teaching tools. I would suggest naming the chords of the arpeggios in the A section. You will see that it follows a pattern of I-IV-V-I. Start by playing block chords followed by the arpeggios. Note that the left hand in the B section plays I and V7. My favorite part is in the left hand of the Coda, where only the bottom note moves for the first five chords. Make sure the last chord is crisp and strong.

RONDO IN CLASSIC STYLE / William Gillock

NFMC 1995-1997

The form of this delightful rondo is clearly defined and simple to analyze: A-B-A^1-C-A^2. It is easy to hear that the A section returns frequently. In the key of G Major, the right hand plays a single-note melodic line, and only in the last two measures do proper chords appear! The fragmented runs from the G Major scale are fun to play and fit well under the hands. Students and teachers have enjoyed this well-crafted piece for decades, and it is an excellent first introduction to rondo form.

WHIRLWIND! / Eric Baumgartner

NFMC 2004-2006

We usually think of a whirlwind as a windstorm but the term may also be used to describe a flurry of activity. What images come to mind as you play this lively and dynamic piece? A fast tempo (feeling the meter 'in two') will help keep things moving, but the key to a strong musical performance is dynamics. Notice how the opening and closing phrases swell and diminish (gusts of wind, perhaps?). Strive for smooth, even control of the eighth notes as you experiment with dynamic subtlety, especially in the *forte* section.

Going Baroque

for Lois Bellm

Glenda Austin

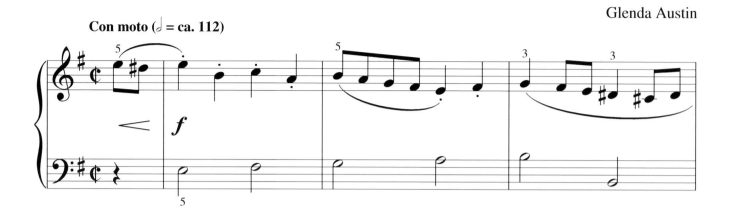

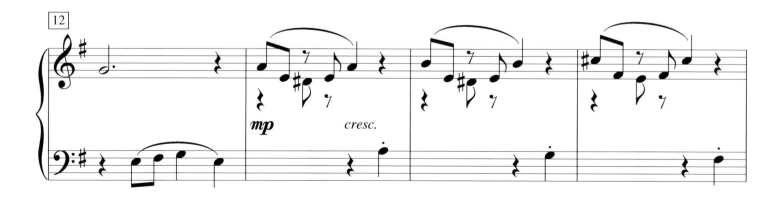

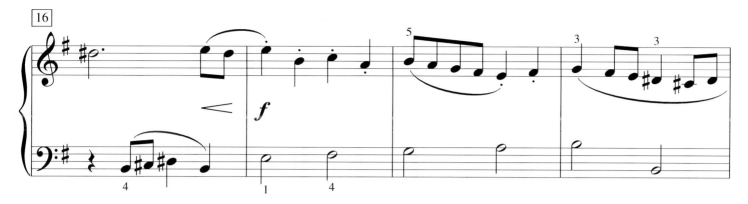

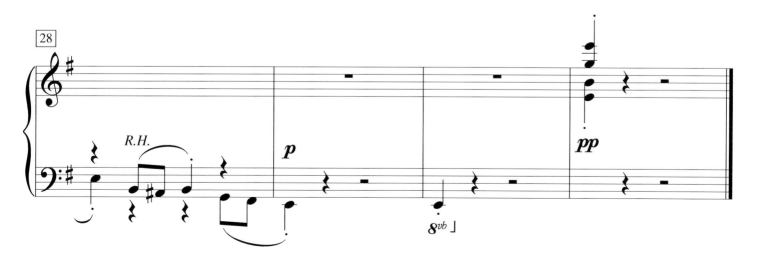

Evening Lament

Randall Hartsell

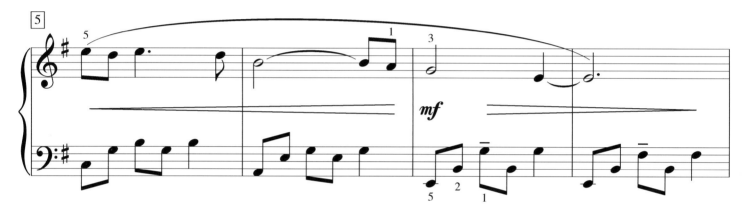

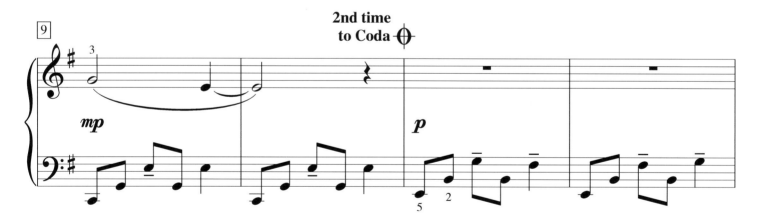

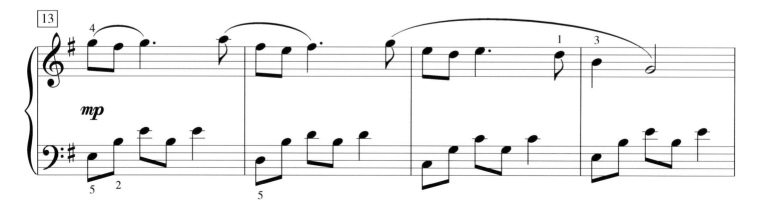

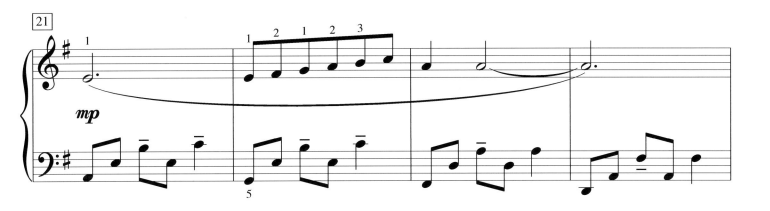

D.C. al Coda

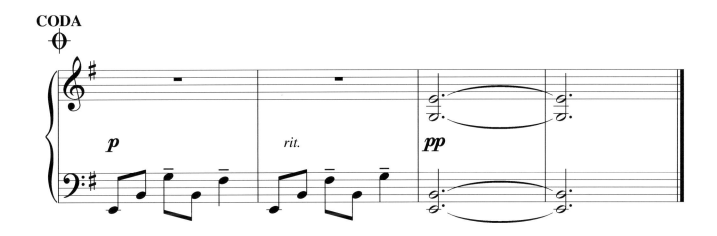

On the Champs-Élysées

for Glenda Austin

William Gillock

With a steady dance beat and minimal rhythmic nuance

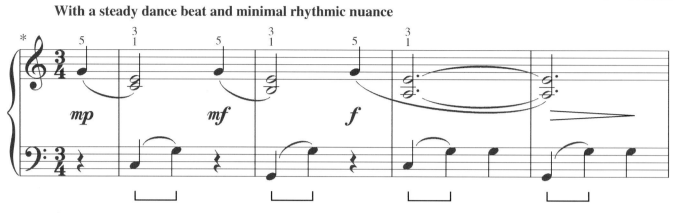

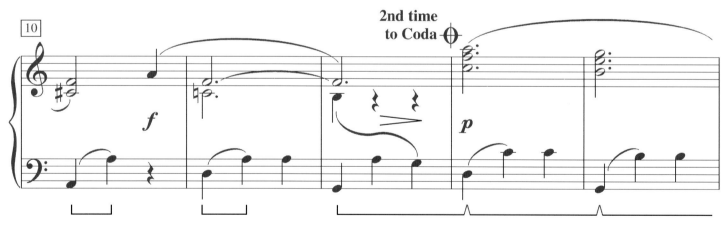

* Original key D-flat Major.

D.C. al Coda

CODA

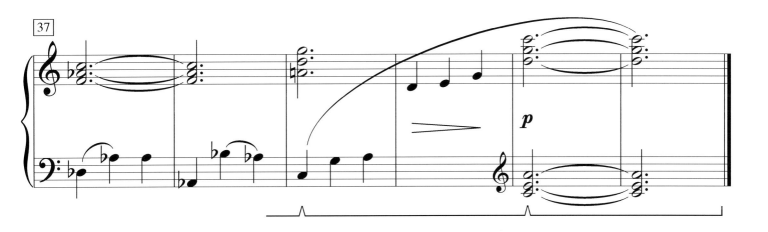

Little Waltz

Carolyn Miller

2nd time to Coda ⊕

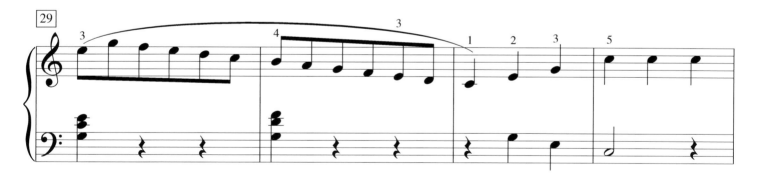

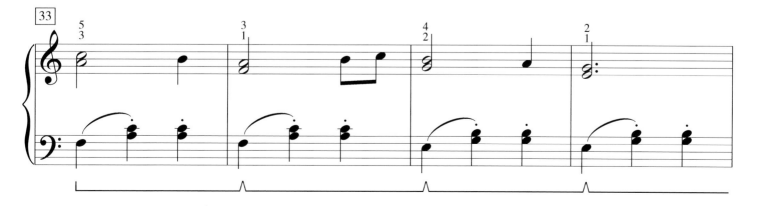

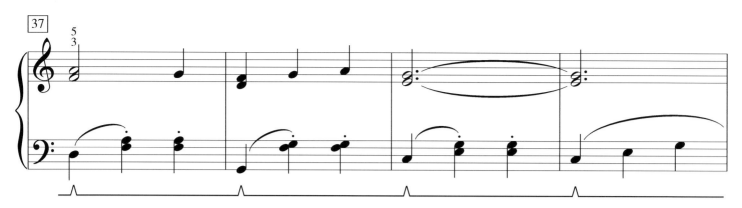

D.S. al Coda

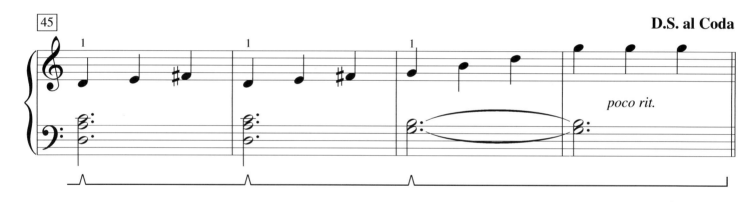

CODA

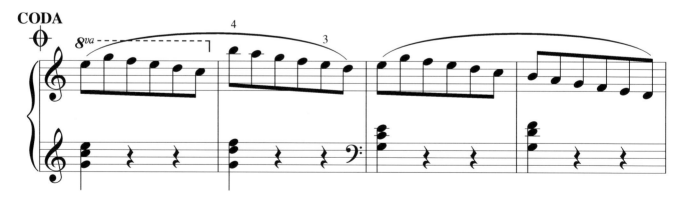

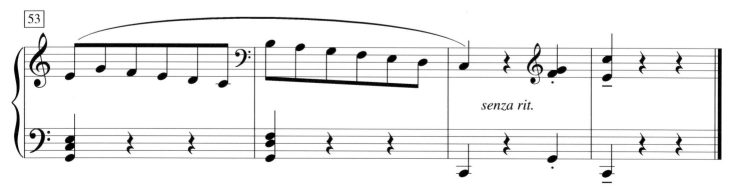

Fountain Square

Eric Baumgartner

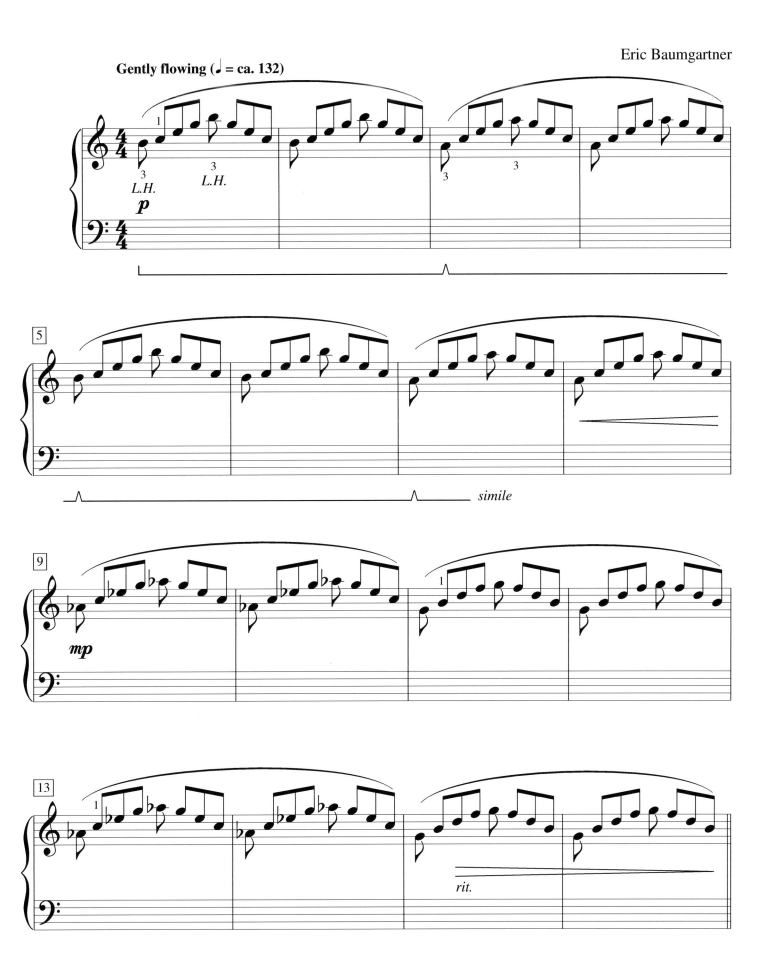

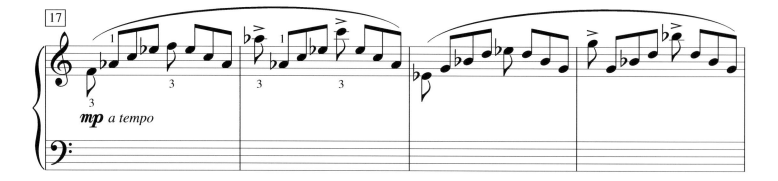

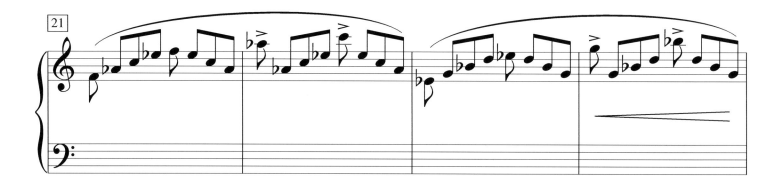

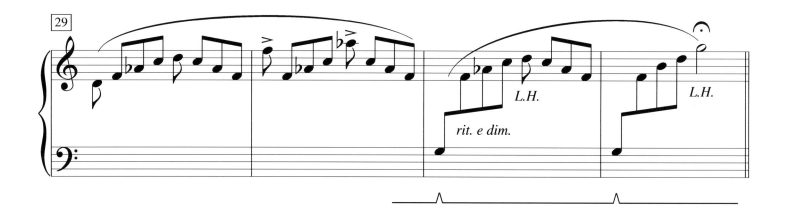

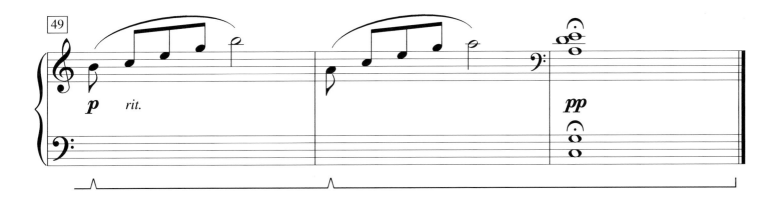

Black Cat Bounce

for Sarah Elizabeth Austin

Glenda Austin

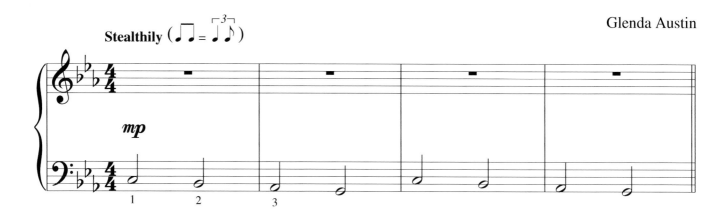

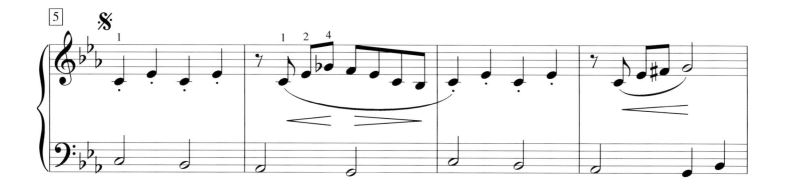

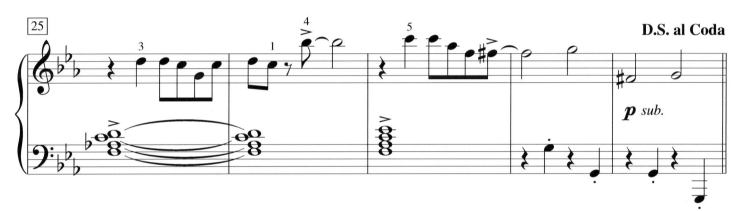

Wistful Chant

Alexander Peskanov
Revised and edited by David Engle*

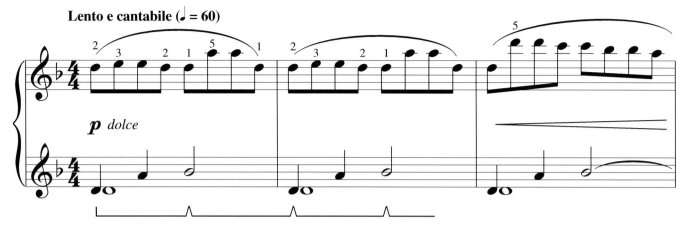

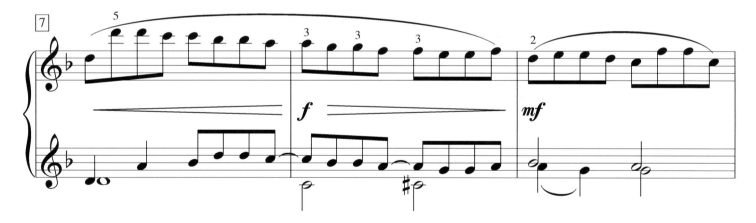

* Refers to original printing.

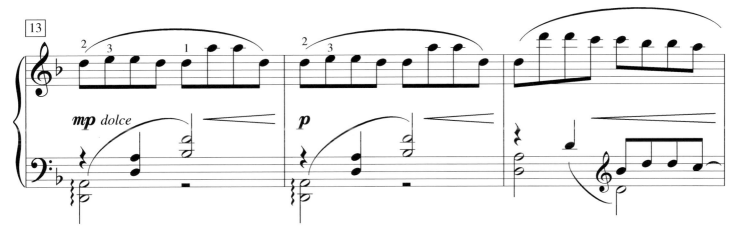

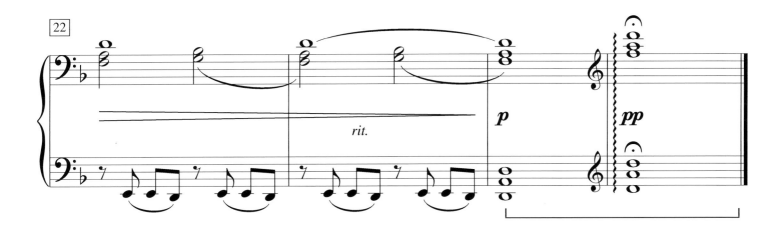

Dance in E Minor

Carolyn Miller
Edited by David Engle*

Allegro moderato

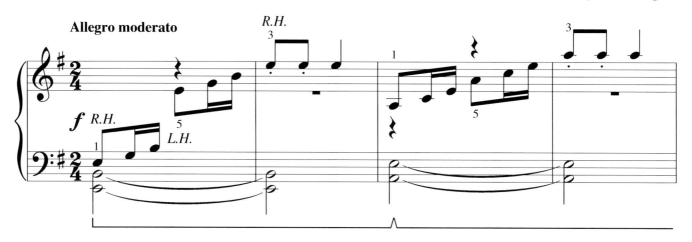

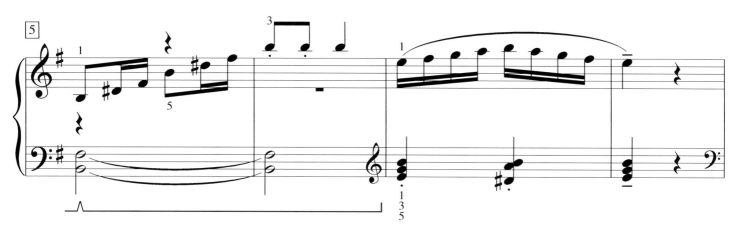

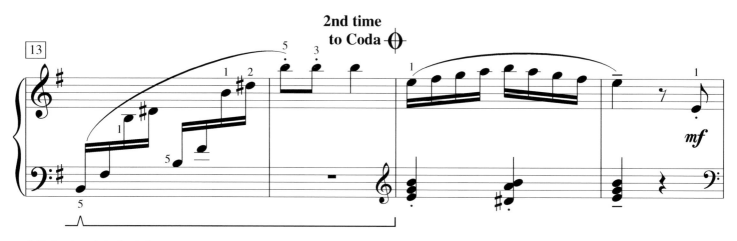

* Refers to original printing.

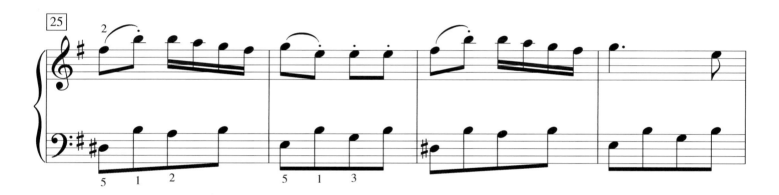

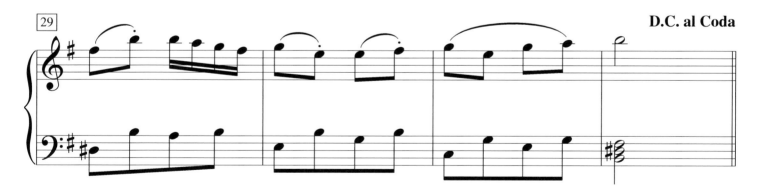

D.C. al Coda

CODA

mp

f

Rondo in Classic Style

William Gillock

Allegro vivace

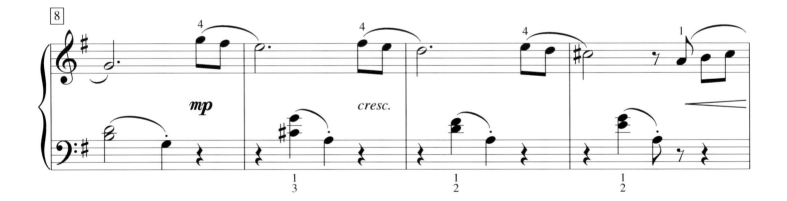

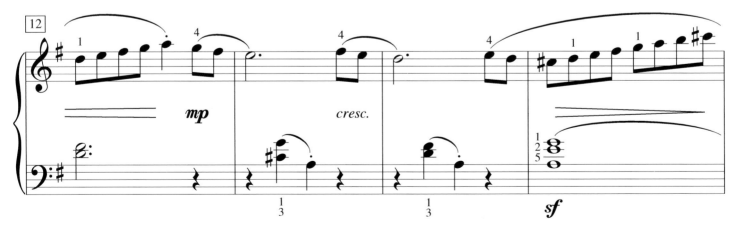

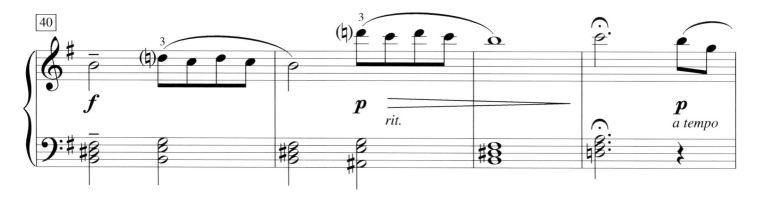

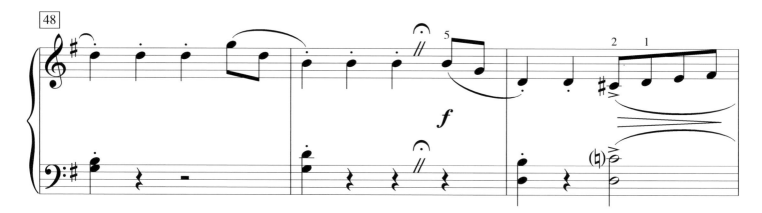

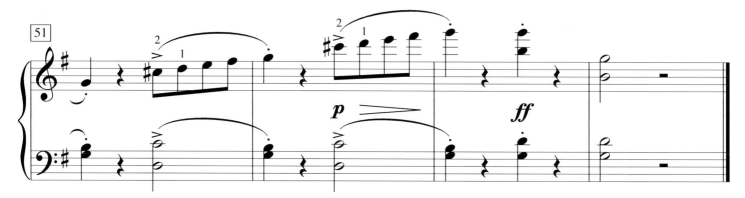

Whirlwind!

Eric Baumgartner

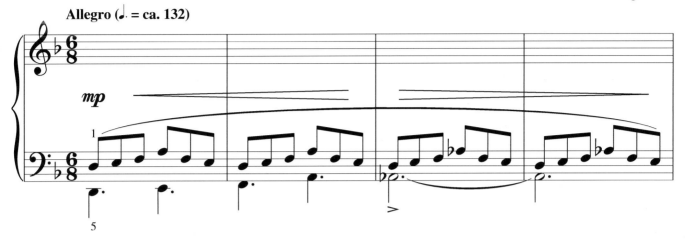

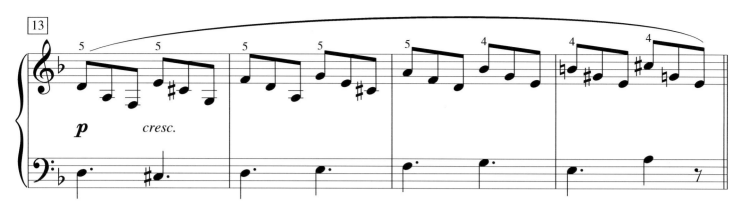

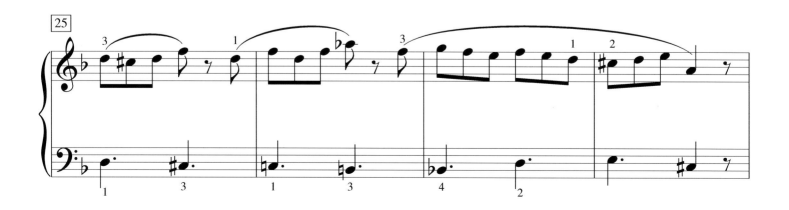

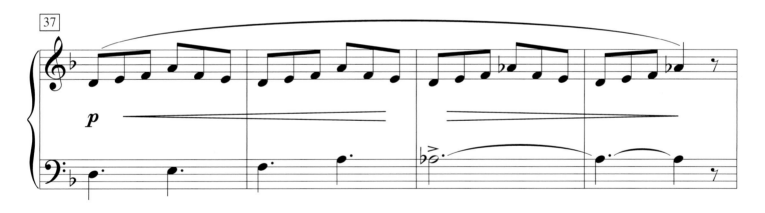

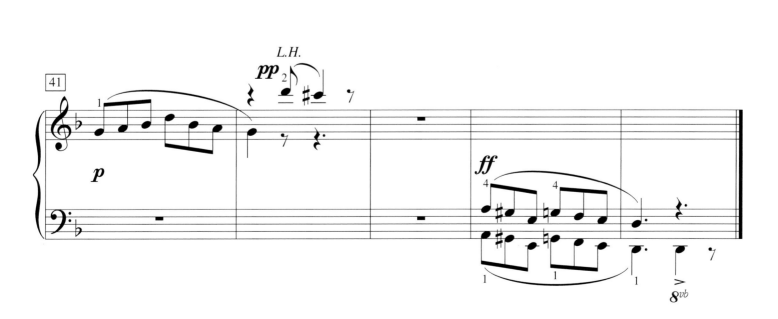

CLASSIC PIANO REPERTOIRE
from Willis Music

The *Classic Piano Repertoire* series includes popular as well as lesser-known pieces from a select group of composers out of the Willis piano archives. Every piece has been newly engraved and edited with the aim to preserve each composer's original intent and musical purpose.

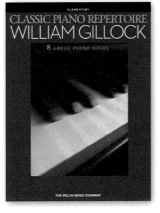

WILLIAM GILLOCK – ELEMENTARY LEVEL
8 Great Piano Solos
Dance in Ancient Style • Little Flower Girl of Paris • On a Paris Boulevard • Rocking Chair Blues • Sliding in the Snow • Spooky Footsteps • A Stately Sarabande • Stormy Weather.

00416957 ....$8.99

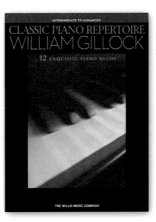

WILLIAM GILLOCK – INTERMEDIATE TO ADVANCED LEVEL
12 Exquisite Piano Solos
Classic Carnival • Etude in A Major (The Coral Sea) • Etude in E Minor • Etude in G Major (Toboggan Ride) • Festive Piece • A Memory of Vienna • Nocturne • Polynesian Nocturne • Sonatina in Classic Style • Sonatine • Sunset • Valse Etude.

00416912 .... $12.99

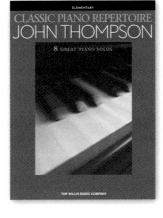

EDNA MAE BURNAM – ELEMENTARY LEVEL
8 Great Piano Solos
The Clock That Stopped • The Friendly Spider • A Haunted House • New Shoes • The Ride of Paul Revere • The Singing Cello • The Singing Mermaid • Two Birds in a Tree.

00110228 ....$8.99

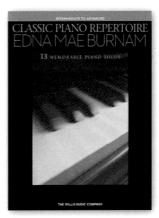

EDNA MAE BURNAM – INTERMEDIATE TO ADVANCED LEVEL
13 Memorable Piano Solos
Butterfly Time • Echoes of Gypsies • Hawaiian Leis • Jubilee! • Longing for Scotland • Lovely Senorita • The Mighty Amazon River • Rumbling Rumba • The Singing Fountain • Song of the Prairie • Storm in the Night • Tempo Tarantelle • The White Cliffs of Dover.

00110229 .... $12.99

JOHN THOMPSON – ELEMENTARY LEVEL
9 Great Piano Solos
Captain Kidd • Drowsy Moon • Dutch Dance • Forest Dawn • Humoresque • Southern Shuffle • Tiptoe • Toy Ships • Up in the Air.

00111968 ....$8.99

JOHN THOMPSON – INTERMEDIATE TO ADVANCED LEVEL
12 Masterful Piano Solos
Andantino (from Concerto in D Minor) • The Coquette • The Faun • The Juggler • Lagoon • Lofty Peaks • Nocturne • Rhapsody Hongroise • Scherzando in G Major • Tango Carioca • Valse Burlesque • Valse Chromatique.

00111969 .... $12.99

EXCLUSIVELY DISTRIBUTED BY

CLOSER LOOK View sample pages and hear audio excerpts online at www.halleonard.com

www.willispianomusic.com

www.facebook.com/willispianomusic

Prices, content, and availability subject to change without notice.

0113

MUSIC FROM
William Gillock

Available exclusively from WILLIS MUSIC

"The Gillock name spells magic to teachers around the world..."
Lynn Freeman Olson, renowned piano pedagogue

NEW ORLEANS JAZZ STYLES

Gillock believed that every student's musical education should include experiences in a variety of popular stylings, including jazz, as a recurring phase of his or her studies. Students should also be encouraged to deviate from the written notes with their own improvisations if desired, for spontaneity is an essential ingredient of the jazz idiom.

Originals

NEW ORLEANS JAZZ STYLES
00415931 Book Only...$4.99

MORE NEW ORLEANS JAZZ STYLES
00415946 Book Only...$4.99

STILL MORE NEW ORLEANS JAZZ STYLES
00404401 Book Only...$4.99

NEW ORLEANS JAZZ STYLES - COMPLETE
00416922 Book/CD..$19.99

Duets (arr. Glenda Austin)

NEW ORLEANS JAZZ STYLES DUETS
00416805 Book/CD...$9.99

MORE NEW ORLEANS JAZZ STYLES DUETS
00416806 Book/CD...$9.99

STILL MORE NEW ORLEANS JAZZ STYLES DUETS
00416807 Book/CD...$9.99

Simplified (arr. Glenda Austin)

SIMPLIFIED NEW ORLEANS JAZZ STYLES
00406603 ....$5.99

MORE SIMPLIFIED NEW ORLEANS JAZZ STYLES
00406604 ....$5.99

STILL MORE SIMPLIFIED NEW ORLEANS JAZZ STYLES
00406605 ....$5.99

ACCENT ON GILLOCK SERIES
Excellent piano solos in all levels by Gillock. Great recital pieces!
00405993	Volume 1 Book	$4.99
00405994	Volume 2 Book	$4.99
00405995	Volume 3 Book	$4.99
00405996	Volume 4 Book	$4.99
00405997	Volume 5 Book	$4.99
00405999	Volume 6 Book	$4.99
00406000	Volume 7 Book	$4.99
00406001	Volume 8 Book	$4.99

"ACCENT ON" SERIES
Selections of original early to mid-intermediate level piano solos, each with a specific pedagogical focus.

ACCENT ON CLASSICAL
Early to Mid-Intermediate Level
Gillock transformed several classical favorites into accessible teaching pieces, including Beethoven's "Für Elise" and "German Dance" (Op.17/9). Other pieces in this timeless collection include: Capriccietto • Barcarolle • Piece in Classic Style • Sonatina in C.
00416932 ....$7.99

ACCENT ON DUETS
Mid to Later Intermediate Level
Eight fantastic Gillock duets in one book! Includes: Sidewalk Cafe • Liebesfreud (Kreisler) • Jazz Prelude • Dance of the Sugar Plum Fairy (Tchaikovsky) • Fiesta Mariachi. A must-have for every piano studio.
00416804 1 Piano/4 Hands...............................$12.99

00415712	Accent on Analytical Sonatinas	EI	$4.99
00415797	Accent on Black Keys	MI	$3.95
00415748	Accent on Majors	LE	$4.95
00415569	Accent on Majors & Minors	EI	$4.99
00415165	Accent on Rhythm & Style	MI	$3.95

CLOSER LOOK

Visit **www.halleonard.com** for score pages and full length audio on most titles.

Type the 8-digit product code in the "Search" field

SEARCH	GO ▸

for fast and easy access.

ALSO AVAILABLE

FOUNTAIN IN THE RAIN
A sophisticated Gillock classic! Composed in 1960, this piece is reminiscent of impressionism and continues to be on annual recital lists. Students particularly enjoy the changing harmonies and nailing the splashy cadenza in the middle!
00414908...$2.99

PORTRAIT OF PARIS
This beautiful composition evokes the romance of long-ago Paris, its eighth notes building gracefully to an incredibly satisfying climax of cascading notes. Excellent for bringing out top-voicing. Gillock has also written a second piano part that results in a very effective piano duo arrangement. (Second Piano Part: 00416293)
00414627...$2.99

THREE JAZZ PRELUDES
These preludes may be played as a set or as individual pieces. These dazzling pieces are Gillock at his best.
00416100...$3.95

CLASSIC PIANO REPERTOIRE – WILLIAM GILLOCK
Intermediate to Advanced
12 beautiful Gillock pieces have been re-engraved in this new collection that is guaranteed to be well-worn in no time! Includes favorites such as *Valse Etude, Festive Piece, Polynesian Nocturne,* and *Sonatine.*
00416912..$12.99

CLASSIC PIANO REPERTOIRE – WILLIAM GILLOCK
Elementary Level
8 great Gillock solos have been re-engraved in this brand new collection. Includes • Little Flower Girl of Paris • Spooky Footsteps • On a Paris Boulevard • Stately Sarabande • Rocking Chair Blues • and more!
00416957..$8.99

Prices, contents, and availability subject to change without notice.

Find us online at
www.willispianomusic.com

www.facebook.com/willispianomusic

WILLIS MUSIC

FOR MORE INFORMATION, SEE YOUR LOCAL MUSIC DEALER, OR WRITE TO:

HAL•LEONARD® CORPORATION
7777 W. BLUEMOUND RD. P.O. BOX 13819 MILWAUKEE, WI 53213

0412